WINDOWBOXES
INDOORS & OUT

100 Projects & Planting Ideas for All Four Seasons

JAMES CRAMER & DEAN JOHNSON

With MARY SEARS Photography by GRIDLEY & GRAVES

Storey Publishing

*The mission of Storey Publishing is to serve our customers by publishing practical
information that encourages personal independence in harmony with the environment.*

Interior design by Susi Oberhelman
Cover design by Wendy Palitz
Cover photographs by Gridley & Graves

First paperback edition published by Storey Publishing 2003.
Hardcover edition originally published as *Window Boxes (Indoors & Out)*
by Artisan, a division of Workman Publishing Company, Inc., 108 Broadway,
New York, New York 10003.

PAGE 11: Lyrics from an old song, as mentioned in Roy E. Biles, *The Modern
Family Garden Book* (Chicago: J. G. Ferguson Publisher, 1935).

PRINTED IN SINGAPORE BY IMAGO

10 9 8 7 6 5 4 3 2 1

Library of Congress Cataloging-in-Publication Data

Cramer, James (James Edward)
  Window boxes indoors & out: 100 projects & planting ideas for all four seasons
: / by James Cramer and Dean Johnson.
      p. cm.
  Includes index.
  ISBN 1-58017-518-X (pbk. : alk. paper)
  1. Window gardening. I. Johnson, Dean. II. Title.
SB419 .C645 2004
635.9'678—dc21
                                              2003012690

TO ELIJAH

Our tears water the flowers

CONTENTS

He has no yard behind his house,
No garden green to till,
And so he works the hothouse plan
Upon his window sill.

I N   E A R L Y   S P R I N G   before we make our first trip to the nursery, we always say we're not going to buy too much. We remind ourselves that we have plenty of plants in the garden and most of them just haven't come up yet. Then we get in the van and pick up our friend Rosita, who's been gardening for most of her seventy-three years. When we get to the nursery we fan out in all directions. Rosita's got her list and we've got ours. When we get back together, pulling our wagons full of flowers, the comparisons start. And so does the trouble. Whatever Rosita finds, we have to have, and vice versa. We all end up buying much more than we have room for. Every year when we're driving home we always say the same thing: We look like a greenhouse on wheels, the back of the van piled high with bushes, plants, seeds, and bags of potting soil and peat moss. There's barely room for the three of us.

In early spring we prowl the local nursery for old favorites like impatiens and anything that's new. Above: Dean snags a Green Prophecy iris for the perennial border in our herb garden. Below: With so much to choose from, it's hard to decide what to take home.

When we get home, we divide things up. Some plants are for the gardens, others are for the window boxes, and some will start out in the window boxes and then move to the gardens later, where they'll have plenty of room to spread.

We've always had gardens, for as long as we can remember, no matter where we've lived. For years we've watched them grow, dividing and rearranging plants the same way we move furniture in the house.

When we bought Seven Gates, here in the westernmost corner of Maryland, we planted gardens long before giving a thought to all the interior work that needed doing. Fifteen years later, we have a formal herb garden, a thriving vegetable garden, a

rose garden, and a garden that changes with the seasons: weeping cherries and tulips in the springtime; lavender, irises, and thistles in the summer; fall grasses and millet in autumn; and stalks of thistles and grasses in the dead of winter.

And we have always planted window boxes. When we've had our fill of double-digging, transplanting, weeding, and dragging the hose around, we turn to our window boxes and relax. Deadheading spent blossoms and watering takes less than a minute. And if you get tired of the way a window box looks, you just pop in something new. Some people have no room for a fully developed garden and it takes time and energy to tend even the smallest plot. With a window box you get a slice of the same effect with far less effort.

Above and below: Marigolds and dogwood proclaim spring's arrival. Opposite: Some of the plants we bought last spring, in one of a half-dozen wagons we fill during a trip through the nursery's greenhouses.

Every time we put a new building on our property, we try to add some kind of window box; it just seems to make a building more friendly and inviting. Many of the boxes at Seven Gates are the traditional rectangular shape, but we're not shy about christening anything that holds dirt a window box. Buckets, basins, straw hats, baskets—all have been pressed into service in the name of capital improvement.

As far as we're concerned, anything that grows is a candidate for a window box. We plant what we like, and we experiment. Taking a risk isn't very risky in a small space; we would never have discovered chartreuse geraniums and rainbow Swiss chard if it weren't for our friend Melanie at the local greenhouse, who is always growing the latest thing.

These "gardens in miniature," from the simplest to the lush, never fail to give abundant pleasure. We may go antiquing and come home empty-handed because we can't find exactly what we were looking for. But if we stop at the nursery we always find something that pleases. So get going. Get planting. Green up your window on the world.

JAMES AND DEAN

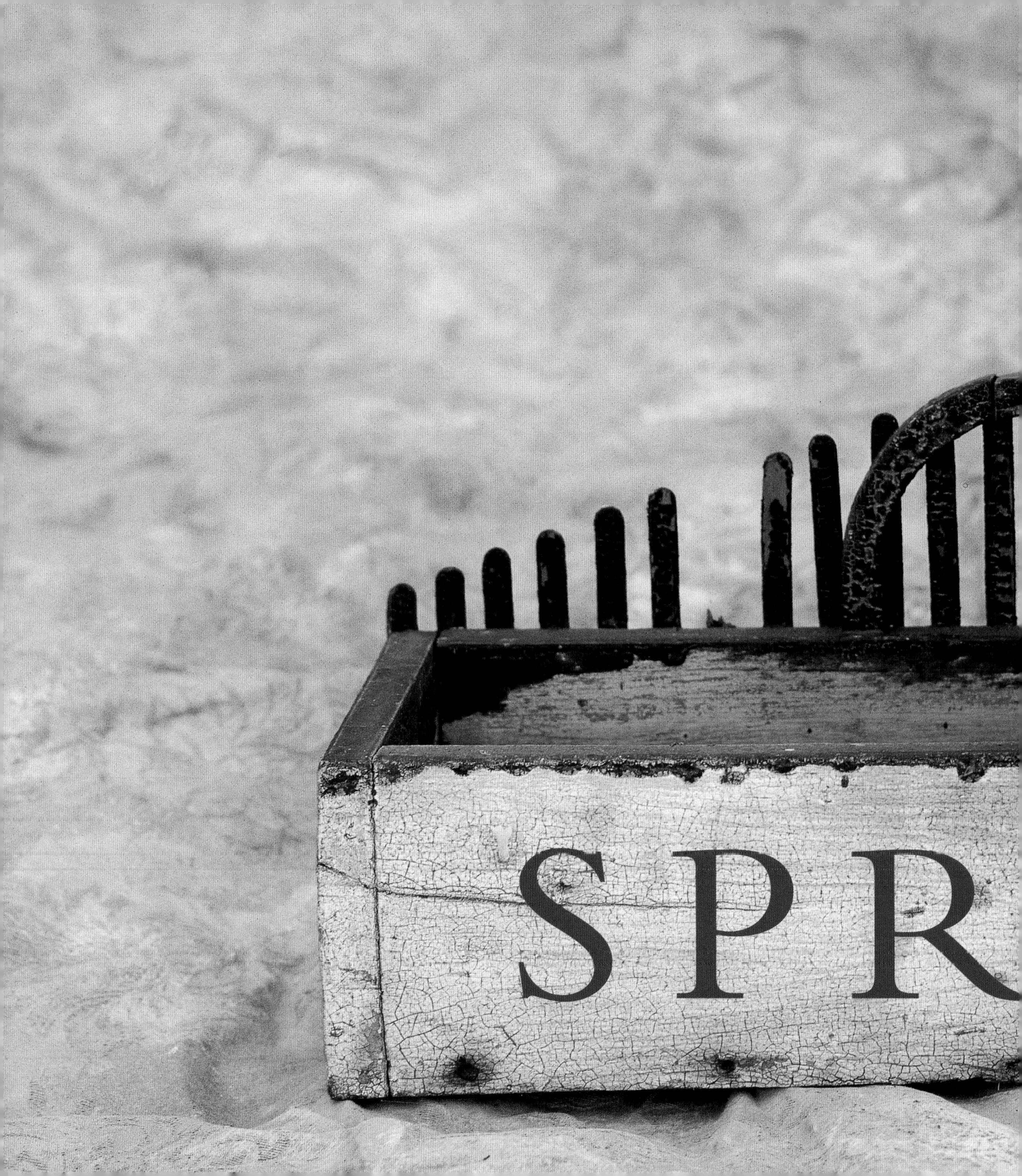
SPR

SPRING PLANTS

rye grass

pansies

tulips

daffodils

crocuses

primroses

lilies of the valley

violas

Johnny-jump-ups

sage

thyme

rosemary

basil

sweet william

lettuce

dianthus

Delicate primroses, above, and bearded irises, below, are unmistakable signs of spring. Opposite: In a window box made from an old iron window grate are Osteospermum daisies—Lusaka, Sonja, and Volta—Joan Wilder nemesia, and clove-scented stock. Johnny-jump-ups bloom in the cold frame.

NEW BEGINNINGS

COOL WINDS USHER IN SPRING, with a fresh new-grass smell that gets stronger after it rains. In our fifteenth season at Seven Gates Farm, there are changes all around. A new aviary in the white garden, eight feet tall with a peaked tin roof, houses four white doves that live in avian splendor, splashing in a stone birdbath and running through the sprinkler. The chicken house is another addition, home to Elvis, Priscilla, Lisa Marie, an unnamed white rooster, and Gladys. (We gave away the Pips.) We built another barn behind the smokehouse to use as a potting shed and photography studio.

The season never seems to make its debut fast enough, so the outdoor furniture comes out of storage long before it's really warm enough for us to sit outside. There's a flea market atmosphere the day tables and chairs tumble out of the smokehouse, resuming their positions on the lawn like seasoned actors on a stage. Some pieces are recast in new roles: Last year's chair becomes this year's plant stand, fuchsias and begonias are potted in an old soup tureen, and the theater of the outdoors begins anew.

Friends who visit Seven Gates Farm all have the impression that we've created our own little world here, and in many ways they're right. This one-acre patch of land is bordered by tall pine trees, and within are gardens, animals, good things growing, and something beautiful wherever you look. We want to send a message that wonderful things happen here, and a large part of that message is conveyed through plants and flowers.

When we first moved here in 1984, we dug our gardens even before we started on the house, and the same set of priorities guides us today. Each trip to the nursery sends us home with more than enough to fill our window boxes and outdoor containers, with plenty left over for the garden and greenhouse. The spring

bulbs planted in both the window boxes and the gardens put on a showy display soon after the snow melts; once the bulbs in the boxes are spent, we pull them out, leaving the foliage intact so it continues to feed them, and store them in dry sand, safe from varmints. (In the fall, we replant the bulbs in window boxes in the cold frame, and thus the cycle repeats itself.)

The vegetable garden gets bigger every year—blame it on the strawberries, with their irrepressible runners. (Eventually we'll have to rename the garden so it accurately reflects its contents!) Meanwhile, the rhubarb fans out, and we feast on fresh asparagus from a farmstand down the road, where payment is by the honor system (you put your money in a jar) and everything—asparagus, broccoli, radishes, garlic, butter lettuce, leeks, peas, spinach, tomato juice in jars, a relish made of squash, onions, and cucumbers that's delicious with ham, and homemade pickled beets—is fresher, cheaper, and more delicious than anything you'd find in a store.

Symbols of spring and the earth's rebirth: Above left: a nest of eggs and lettuce; above right: eggs tiered on a graceful stand; opposite: miniature roses.

Simple plantings make a spirited showing. Above left: Creeping Jenny takes hold in a terra-cotta pot collared by a metal ring. Planting in pairs gives a more formal impression; this pot has a twin on the other side of the window. Above right: Daisies and sweet potato vines make a cheery combination. Opposite: Salmon-colored phlox of sheep—a fluffy flower with an amusing play on words for a name—finds a home on a weathered 1950s garden chair in the same tones.

In late spring we mix more potting soil, head back to the nursery for unusual plants and succulents for the hot dry days ahead, and replace worn-out pansies with drought-resistant flowers such as geraniums, nasturtiums, and Supertunias, a type of petunia that blooms all summer.

The season ends with our annual trip to Reinholds, Pennsylvania, for Ned and Gwen Foltz's flowerpot show. Ned makes redware pottery, and on one particular weekend (usually the last of April) the Foltzes have an open house, one of seven they hold each year. They invite a small group of artists to show their wares in Ned's studio, a converted stone schoolhouse built in 1860. Dean takes his cloches, window boxes, and greenhouses, Ned sells flowerpots, Gwen cooks up a storm, and everyone eats, talks, and sells for two days straight. It's a big family get-together, and as we drive home we're reminded that our "family" includes not just blood relatives, but all those who have come to mean so much to us over the years.

STARTING SEEDS

STARTING SEEDS INDOORS is a great way to get a jump on spring. We're lucky to have a greenhouse, but a sunny windowsill does a fine job, too. Plant your seeds in terra-cotta seed trays, peat pots, egg cartons, or plastic seed trays, which work especially well because they hold moisture. Any container should be two to three inches deep with drainage holes in the bottom. Moisten the soil, then poke holes in the dirt using a pencil and insert seeds one at a time.

Use a light soil that's kind to newborn roots and gradually acclimate plants to sunlight at a south-facing window. Remember to rotate the containers every three days to keep young plants from bending toward the light. Give the plants a chance to "harden off" by putting them outside in filtered sun for a few hours a day.

Soil Mixture

4 cups peat moss
2 cups perlite
2 cups vermiculite

This recipe makes a light soil that holds moisture but won't crush tender roots. Use for starting plants.

Opposite: A copper-lined greenhouse on legs is made in the style of a cold frame but set indoors to nurture young plants. The lining holds water and reflects the sun's rays, and the lid opens to control humidity. Drawers are handy for garden tools and broken crockery, which can be recycled to partially plug drain holes in flowerpots.

When outdoor temperatures are sufficiently warm and plants are large enough, plant your window box. Drill or cut holes in the bottom of the box for drainage and line the bottom with a few stones, pieces of broken clay pot, or lightweight Styrofoam peanuts for aeration. Fill the box with spring soil mixture (page 28) to within three inches of the top. Add the plants, loosening the root balls before positioning each in the soil. Then continue to add soil to within an inch of the top of the box. Follow with a fine misting of water, then add more soil as the soil settles. Water the plants regularly, whenever the surface soil feels dry.

We always start this process with a trip to the nursery to buy the basics—impatiens, geraniums, begonias, salvia, verbena, and herbs—and look for new and unusual plants such as hellebores and wallflowers. We also order from specialty catalogs; this year we chose black krim tomatoes, red arrow broccoli, purple sweet peas, black cornflowers, agrostemma (a tall white border flower with speckled black markings), and valerian St. George, a perennial.

Opposite: Although it looks old, this potting table with a greenhouse top and copper liner was made by Dean from scratch. (The concrete chickens standing guard are optional.) Inside, miniature marigolds gain a foothold (detail above right) along with lettuce, cabbage, and tomatoes. Once the seedlings have established themselves, they're ready to be transplanted to a window box. Seeds started in egg carton sections or in peat pots (sold at garden centers) can be placed directly in the soil.

One-Two-Three Window Boxes

Instead of loading up your window box with seven or eight different plants, simplify with a one-, two-, or three-plant plan.

1 THE ONE-PLANT WINDOW BOX is the newest look. A single row of identical plants, lined up like soldiers, creates a simple, clean, and airy effect.

2 THE TWO-PLANT WINDOW BOX, somewhere between spare and lush, gives plants room to breathe and grow. Put tall plants in back and low, bushy plants in front—you can never go wrong with this high-low effect.

3 THE THREE-PLANT WINDOW BOX is tightly packed for a lush English look. Plant in three rows like a class picture: trailing plants in the front row, medium-height plants in the middle, and taller plants in the back.

SPRING
BOXES

Soil Mixture

4 cups potting soil
2 cups perlite
2 cups vermiculite
4 cups peat moss
2 tablespoons blood meal
1 tablespoon gypsum

Once your plants are established, transplant them to this spring soil mix, which is rich yet light enough for a window box. It holds moisture, but won't get too heavy when the soil gets wet. Gypsum looks like sand, and helps to break down soil; it can also be used to lighten the clay soil in your garden.

WHATEVER THE ARRANGEMENT, a window box should have a harmonious air, with all the elements blending into a unified whole. Achieving that end requires a delicate balance. Too many different plants overwhelm the eye. Too few and the arrangement looks stingy. And if one plant sinks, the entire box goes down. We've always believed that modest, unpretentious boxes are the prettiest. Our advice: Aim for simplicity.

A grouping should have a dominant color scheme, even if that scheme calls for many colors. Flowers and foliage in eye-catching shades make a box unique. In the last two years we've been using a lot of lime-colored foliage to give the boxes a lift. The light leaves make a nice contrast with dark foliage.

Line up your plants at the nursery; put colors side by side to see how they relate; choose foliage as well as flowers. If you're planting from seeds, consider the plants' eventual size, which you can judge from the statistics or photograph on the seed packet. Pair plants that need similar amounts of water and sun, but don't shy away from unusual combinations. Plants are more adaptable than you think.

Opposite: Imperial Antique pansies bloom up a storm in a range of pastels from soft pink to butter yellow. The picket-fence window box is made of wood salvaged from an old painted shutter. Creeping Pulegiodies thyme peeks through the pickets, and dwarf curry, a lacy, silvery-white herb with leaves resembling lavender, grows in back.

Make sure the window box is deep enough for roots to grow. It should be as wide as the window, if not wider, and should be in proportion to the window and the building. When in doubt, it's better to go too large than too small.

Display a mix of textures. A blend of soft, spiky, and feathery elements keeps the eye amused. Herbs are a good way to inject texture because they have such varied leaves, and they flower in surprising ways.

Have a shape in mind before you start; it gives the arrangement some structure. A sketch will help make your ideas concrete. Some of the plants should stand tall and others should hang down. Create a triangular effect with tall plants in the middle and lower plants on either side, or set tall plants on each side and mound puffy plants in between for a swooping shape. Try twisted vines, ivy, cascading blossoms, slender-stemmed flowers—each creates a different skyline. Remember to include some trailing plants; the most common mistake is to have all the plants growing upward, with nothing to balance them down below. The window above the window box can also be framed with plants to add another architectural element to the mix.

Opposite: Just about any decorative piece can be cast as a window box. This handmade arbor with porch baluster columns and a pergola-style top is a bird feeder in summer, but off season it's a window "box" brimming with ivy and roses. Primroses line the sill. Above right: Harmonizing colors are guaranteed to boost interest. In this salmon-painted window box attached to the kitchen door, pink English primroses meet their match in English lustreware plates.

Easy Installation

To mount a window box on brackets, fasten the brackets to the framework of the window four inches from each end of the box. Use brass, stainless steel, or galvanized screws, which won't rust.

To mount a box directly on the house, position it below the windowsill and screw through the back into the sill.

A box can also sit right on a windowsill if the sill is deep enough. Secure the box by wiring it to the window frame using strong wire attached to eye hooks screwed into the frame and the front corners of the box.

To prevent the siding or sill from rotting, leave a one-inch air space between the window box and the house so that air can circulate. Use small wooden blocks, or raise the box on terra-cotta feet, which are sold at garden centers.

Plants to Flatter Your Home

FOR A FORMAL HOUSE,
fill window boxes with dramatic plants
that have a definite shape: small dwarf
Alberta spruce, ivy, hosta, caladium,
dwarf boxwood, daffodils, tulips. Paint the
boxes the same color as the house
trim or shutters. Place a pair of tapering
plant stands on either side of the front
door to underscore the symmetry.

FOR A RUSTIC HOUSE, fill
window boxes with fluffy irregular plants:
vinca, lobelia, black-eyed Susans, maidenhair
fern, trailing snapdragons, zinnias, old-
fashioned varieties of flowers. Use
weathered wooden boxes, or paint boxes
in several gradations of the same color,
with the darker ones on the bottom story,
and the lightest at the top. Place concrete
troughs and urns filled with similar
flowers and foliage outside the house.

FOR A VICTORIAN COTTAGE,
fill brightly painted window boxes or wire
boxes to overflowing with multicolored
flowers: violets, phlox, cosmos, Boston fern,
petunias, nasturtiums, lavender. Decorate
the front porch with potted begonias on a
metal plant stand with outstretched arms.

Hot yellows, oranges, and purples can be toned down with light foliage such as lamb's ears, dusty miller, silver thyme, sage, and silver mound artemesia. Blue, pink, white, and mauve have a cool effect, shown off beautifully against dark foliage such as ferns, hosta, sweet potato vines, purple basil, black grass, or begonias. **Opposite: A dough box brims with Solar coleus, chartreuse geraniums, and salmon tulips on a back porch where bittersweet climbs.**

Above: In a zinc box, cheerful pansies and violas are set off by moonlight thyme. The Sherbet Lavender Ice violas in the middle will open and turn blue as they mature. Yesterday, Today, and Tomorrow violas stand in back.

EASTER
BOXES

OUT IN THE GREENHOUSE on Palm Sunday we set to work making special holiday window boxes. They're similar to Easter baskets and appeal to kids of all ages. Key ingredients are eggs, straw, cabbages, young lettuce, toy bunnies, ribbons—anything childlike or farmlike that's fragile, small, and pastel. Long, slim galvanized washtubs and baskets are the containers of choice—they'll fit on a windowsill, and can be used as holiday centerpieces. We always grow our own Easter grass—rye grass is quick to germinate—to create a soft bed for decorations. Baskets placed by the front door and on the doorsteps convey a cheery welcome.

Left: A galvanized tub of romaine is edged with "wallpaper eggs," papier-mâché eggs painted sage-green with white designs to resemble old wallpaper patterns. (Let the eggs dry on crumpled plastic so the paint won't peel off when you lift them.) Opposite: Nested in a basket of rye grass, nasturtium seedlings in eggshells are the very essence of spring. Fill the shells with a light soil mixture and one or two seeds, and prick a drainage hole in the bottom with a pin. Plant directly in the ground when the seedlings reach a suitable size, crushing the shell so the roots can emerge.

On a limestone wall near the back door of our friend Rosita's stone house, an Easter basket is bedded down near wild phlox. To make your own, fill a straw-lined wicker basket with Joan Wilder nemesia, a fragrant flower with dark-lavender blossoms that's especially happy in a window box in full sun. Engage the imagination by studding the box with a few well-chosen "props"—in this case, papier-mâché eggs and a chick, both early-nineteenth-century candy containers from Germany.

MAY DAY BOXES

ON MAY DAY, it's traditional to put flowers on the doorsteps of loved ones, ring the doorbell, and run away, leaving them to discover a fistful of just-picked flowers, a nosegay in a paper cone, or a basket of flowers hanging by a ribbon from the doorknob. Sometimes a poem or verse is attached. Try a new twist on the custom by leaving pots of flowering plants at your friends' houses, with instructions for planting them in a window box. Better yet, leave a preplanted window box, all arranged and ready to enjoy, with a word or two on how to take care of it.

Left: Black devil pansies and sweetly scented lilies of the valley make an elegant statement in contrasting colors. Opposite: A trio of painted tin buckets sprouts candytuft, Silver Lady daisies, and variegated lysimachia, soon to sport yellow blossoms. The buckets are linked with wire through holes punched below the lip of each. The one in the middle has a homemade wire handle as well, so the threesome can hang from a gate, fence, or window sill. Overleaf: Three well-worn watering cans filled with Osteospermum daisies parade below a window on an outdoor bench.

Out of the Ordinary

Unusual objects—upturned hats, baskets, tin cans, shopping carts, wooden crates, broken pots, even a birdbath—make great planters. Almost any treasure found at an auction or flea market can be turned into a window box of some sort. If the container isn't waterproof, add a sheet of plastic or a plastic bag to keep the soil from washing away. The container gets more attention if the plantings are simple. Park these portable bouquets on a table or chair in the garden, in a bathroom, or on an outdoor windowsill.

Opposite: Hanging on a garden gate, a trellis box with flaking blue paint bursts with Snow Crystal alyssum. Right: A decorative piece of painted wrought iron with a verdigris finish is a lacy backdrop for a basket of sweet william and candytuft suspended from an antique ribbon.

HERB
BOXES

MINT AND CHIVES are the upstarts of spring—the first herbs to "green up" the garden when mornings are still on the chill side. If they were planted in a window box the year before, they will be the first to make a return appearance in spring. Small flowers planted around herbs, whether in a window box or garden, will keep the herbs company until other plants appear. The two kinds of plants make an arresting combination, especially in bouquets. Violas, pansies, and alyssum are ideal flowers for early spring boxes because they thrive in cool weather.

The more you clip herbs, the bushier they get, so for really lush window boxes, pinch them frequently as the season progresses. Any herb that hasn't taken off can be replaced with a potted herb from the nursery. Or simply remove the slackers to leave room for healthy ones to ramble as their roots run wild. For a few spikes of color at the end of summer, let some herbs go to seed and flower as your other plants are waning.

Left: A spice box houses French cooking herbs: lavender, winter savory, thyme, sage, rosemary, and marjoram. The box will thrive indoors in a sunny window. Opposite: Galvanized buckets are painted white, inscribed with the name of their cargo, and lined up on a kitchen sill. The bottoms were filled with stones before the herbs were added.

Herbs for SUN

basil
dill
bay
thyme
parsley
rosemary
sage
edible marigold
oregano
sweet marjoram

Left: Italian herbs—rosemary, marjoram, oregano, and sage—take up residence in their own terra-cotta planter. Grow them in the sun outside a kitchen door, where they will flourish throughout spring and summer. Clip them as needed for cooking and garnishes.

Herbs for SHADE

bay
comfrey
lemon balm
mint
sorrel
parsley
hops
sweet woodruff
pennyroyal
sweet cicely

Above left: A window box doesn't have to be a four-sided wooden rectangle. This wire topiary chair form hangs from two hooks on the back of a shed, below an open window. Parsley and apricot alyssum spill from a box tucked inside the chair seat. Below left: This little plant barrow relays potted plants around the garden and greenhouse. When it's not in use, it fits under the window as a planter. Based on an old design, the barrow resembles a wooden flat with twelve-inch legs and handles. It's filled with Osmin deep purple basil, edged with spicy globe basil plants, and anchored in each corner by purple- and green-leaved African blue basil. In the center, a myrtle topiary supplies a vertical axis.

Staddle Stone Box

In the past, mushroom-shaped staddle stones were commonly used as building foundations in England. Here, two miniature stones balance a galvanized metal étagère tray, which in turn holds an assortment of herbs in tiny flowerpots. A Stonehenge kind of window box!

MATERIALS

A 60-pound bag of Sakrete sand mix
Wedge-shaped wooden form, lightly nailed together, to mold the flat-topped base
Shallow wooden box of sand, about 2 feet square and 3 inches deep, to mold the mushroom-shaped top
Water

To make one stone (base and top), mix a small portion of mortar according to directions on the bag.

For the base, scoop mortar into the wedge-shaped wooden form, tamping it down slightly with a trowel to remove air pockets and smooth the surface.

For the mushroom-shaped top, dampen the sand in the wooden box with water and with your fingers make a shallow bowl-like depression in the sand. Scoop mortar into the depression, tamping and smoothing as above, so the top will have a smooth underside when it dries.

Let the cement set overnight, or until hard. (In damp weather, the cement takes longer to set.) When it's dry, lift the mushroom top from the sand and break the wooden form loose from around base, being careful not to drop them. Balance the mushroom top on the base.

STEP BY STEP

51

SUMMER PLANTS

geraniums

lavender

succulents

impatiens

salvia

petunias

daisies

vegetables

begonias

sweet potato vines

nicotiana

dusty miller

zinnias

verbena

Above: A terra-cotta box filled with German healing onions sits on an old iron bench next to bamboo garden stakes. Below: Stacked on cobblestones, a stone trough in the greenhouse holds extra flowerpots and gazania daisies. Opposite: Succulents are easy care and love the sun.

THE GOOD LIFE

SUMMER IN THIS CORNER of Maryland is much like summer throughout the mid-Atlantic states. The energy of spring throttles down, and the heat of July and August takes over. When we moved to Seven Gates fifteen years ago, there was farmland all around, but development has meant far more houses and far less open land. However, this is still apple country, and fields full of squat and gnarly trees continue to keep company with towns full of eighteenth- and nineteenth-century houses; their solid redbrick and stone facades give a sense of permanence.

For us, the day begins just before sunrise with a wake-up call from the roosters. Through the open door, we can hear the doves' soft cooing from their screened-in home in the white garden. And as the dew dries, we go through the gardens on cruise control, enjoying the look and smell of the flowers and soil, making lazy mental notes of things to do.

The list is short: Water, weed, and feed. The gardens have a mind of their own by now. Everything so carefully planted in spring erupts in full glory, sometimes in reckless ways we hadn't anticipated. Our job is to keep things within bounds.

The window boxes have hit their stride, and need just deadheading to encourage more blooms. Anything that's expired, leggy, or bug ridden gets pulled out, and a few annuals from the nursery are poked in to fill in the blanks. Some of the window boxes miss out on rainfall because of the way they're positioned, so we make sure each one gets enough water; the combination of dryness and heat can ruin a window box faster than anything else.

Then we transplant. The excitement of spring invariably leads to more planted pots, jugs, and urns than we can easily care for, and by midsummer we're weary of watering. So we relocate some plants from their containers to the flower beds, where they

Left: A staircase deserves a window box, like this sophisticated black-and-white mix of impatiens and coleus with underpinnings of lighter green. Above: Daisies, rosy petunias, and dusty miller are a classic combination. Below: Mounds of petunias add a delicious ruffle to a simple window.

Above: Instead of spewing seeds, this old grain drill sprouts Silver Brocade dusty miller and purple verbena. Below: A new silhouette for the window box: free-standing, on legs, and eminently portable. A perforated bottom increases air circulation to the plant roots. Opposite: Potted begonias gather in a hand-forged iron box in the shade of our well. We built the well over an old cistern, adapting the design from one we saw in Williamsburg.

don't need as much attention. But we still make our rounds with the watering cans, hoses, and an extendable watering wand. Every plant gets a drink, sometimes twice a day—early in the morning and a few hours before nightfall—so the leaves have a chance to dry out before dark to discourage rotting and pests.

PEOPLE OFTEN ASK us where we get our inspiration. The answer is twofold: We love to collect old gardening books—when it comes to gardening, the wisdom of yesterday never goes out of style. And we're always looking for new places and ideas to check out.

Being far from our everyday routine always rekindles the imagination. Last summer we spent two weeks visiting gardens in the English countryside. And we spend a fair amount of time in Shepherdstown, West Virginia, just across the border from Seven Gates. Its wealth of eighteenth-century stone houses, charming street scenes, and abundance of window boxes—not to mention the shopping and restaurants—draws us back again and again.

We sketch our gardens so we'll remember how they looked when we're planting the following year. In England we sketched gates and took pictures of plants we hoped to find in America. We don't usually carry a camera, but so often we'll stumble across something—the color of a house, the design of a shutter, an unusual planter—and think "If only we'd brought the camera." Time and again, we've had to resort to "brain snapshots" to remember what we've seen—a risky venture at best, with decidedly mixed results. We vow to bring a camera more often.

In late summer, we feed the window boxes and the gardens with 20-20-20 fertilizer to force the last blooms from the flowers and encourage a final display of color and greenery. Then, as the curtain falls on the season, everything gets a good pruning. We used to do this promptly, bringing on fall as soon as we could. But with every passing year, we're slowing the pace, holding on to the glory of summer for as long as we possibly can.

SUMMER BOXES

A SUMMER WINDOW BOX should be like a summer house: casual and easy care. We tend to augment the spring window boxes with a few more flowers from the nursery, laying out bright annuals like swatches of fabric until we settle on some pleasing combinations. Any plant that runs out of gas is replaced: Off with their heads! becomes our summer mantra, as we deadhead to encourage more blooms. With so many window boxes both inside and outside the house, we feel we're in a garden at every turn.

Coordinating window box plants with the surrounding gardens results in a stylish, cohesive look. Left: This burgeoning box holds golden oregano, Wedgwood thyme, trailing chartreuse sweet potato vines, Scottish moss, white geraniums, and Showy Calla mint. The window is accented by a swath of lace. Harmonizing in the garden below are rosemary, bronze fennel, chartreuse geraniums, chartreuse coleus, and white iceberg roses. Opposite: The same box when it was first planted. Silver Lady white daisies got leggy and were replaced as the season progressed.

Gardener's Tea

Feeding established plants once a month with a weak solution of manure tea will keep window boxes looking bright and healthy.

Outdoors, fill a large bucket or eight-gallon tub with water. Pour two pounds of manure into a burlap bag and tie the top closed. Put the bag in the tub and drape it over the side like a tea bag so the manure steeps in the water. When the solution is the color of strong coffee (this takes about ten days), fill your watering can or bucket halfway, then dilute by adding water until the solution is the color of weak tea. Leave the bag in the tub, adding water as the level drops. The tub can be refilled twice before you have to replace the manure. A solution that's too strong will "burn" the roots of your plants, so don't be fooled into thinking more is better. Be sure to dilute the tea.

This solution is also a fine tonic for the vegetable garden and for flower beds. Always water the roots of the plants, not the foliage, so the leaves don't burn in the hot sun.

Opposite: Our backyard table under the arbor is topped with lace and brightened by a galvanized window box planted with globe amaranth, silver dusty miller, and ageratum. A perfect place to snap beans (left) on a summer afternoon.

Above left: Layering plants of different heights adds dimension to a window box arrangement. Here, low-growing ageratum veils the legs of tall nicotiana in a cedar box along a path in our thyme garden. Below left: Fragile as a bridal bouquet, pink begonias and impatiens hemmed with white alyssum spill from a Nantucket window box cushioned with pink hydrangeas. Opposite: On a bench in front of a spring house, a rusting 1940s bread box gets new life, packed with fuchsias, begonias, and mixed lobelia grown from seed. Holes were punched in the bottom for drainage.

Window Box Care and Feeding

Like all plants in containers, those in window boxes need more attention than plants growing in the earth. A summer box needs constant water and maintenance. We water ours once in the morning when the plants are young, and twice a day as they mature. Annuals are grown to bloom for one season and then die, so if you deadhead your flowers as they bloom, you'll force more to appear. Pinch off growing tips to encourage bushy growth. We're partial to Supertunias, a type of petunia that will continue to bloom all summer.

For high blooms on flowering plants, we also sprinkle time-release fertilizer beads called Osmocote 14-14-14 over the soil about one month after planting, when the plants have had a chance to establish themselves.

If your box sits on a windowsill, don't assume that it will get enough moisture; sometimes overhangs prevent rain from reaching it. Make sure to water outdoor boxes regularly.

Opposite: A wire window box mounted above the bed is filled with a changing array of potted plants. White geraniums and ivy are a crisp combination; petunias and nicotiana would smell delightful at night. Above left: A straw-stuffed hay rack bears an array of leafy herbs. Hay racks are sold at farm supply stores, and garden shops stock similar designs. Above right: Some planters are specially designed to grip the railing of a deck, patio, landing, or porch. This half tub accents the footbridge above a stream in western Maryland.

SUN & SHADE

Soil Mixture

1 cup builder's sand

1 cup potting soil

1 cup perlite

4 cups small stones

This mixture is the perfect medium for growing sun-loving succulents.

THERE'S ALWAYS A PLACE for a window box, no matter how sunny or shady the location. Cacti and succulents are made for intensely sunny areas; we keep a bag of sandy soil premixed in the potting shed so we can create a quick display whenever we come across some interesting new varieties.

Every bit as beautiful are shady glens and nooks, where foliage is more effective than flowers. In fact, the newest thing in gardening today is big foliage, few flowers, and sometimes no flowers at all. The colors of leaves and their shapes and sizes are the focus, and the contrast between dark and light creates a serene effect that's soothing to the eye.

Opposite: Light-loving hens and chicks spill from the sections of a white window box set on a round bistro table outdoors. Succulents are perfect for window boxes because they thrive in full sun with very little supervision.

Plants for
SUN

alyssum
succulents
geraniums
petunias
heliotrope
dusty miller
cosmos
snapdragons
dahlias
nasturtiums

Above: Broken flowerpots make a rustic window box for cactus opuntia and cobweb hens and chicks. Neither plant requires much soil. Below: A mix of succulents, including sedum and hens and chicks, fill this wire window box lined with chicken wire, moss, and a sandy soil mixture. Succulents don't like wet feet and appreciate good drainage. Opposite: A Japanese beech fern, Osmunda purple-stemmed royal ferns, and arrow plants thrive in an oak-splint berry basket. The prettiest, lushest shade boxes look as though they were transplanted from the woods. This basket fits the bill, looking suitably rustic outside our back door.

Plants for
SHADE

ferns
begonias
hosta
impatiens
ivy
caladium
violas
violets
mint
philodendron
sweet woodruff
peace lilies

This foliage display has all the attributes of a floral window box and none of the fuss. Pots of Plantaginca aphrodite hosta and white caladium with dark green veins fill a French wire basket hung on the fence. The plants are easy to care for and seek out shade; the contrast of the leaves against the surrounding dark green English ivy is quite dramatic. The August Moon hosta on the metal chair—a 1960s find—needs to grow a bit to join the big leagues in the basket.

SCENT BOXES

WE LIKE TO FILL A WINDOW BOX to overflowing with highly scented plants—old-fashioned roses, heliotrope, night-scented stock, alyssum, scented geraniums, lilies of the valley, carnations, jasmine, and lavender are favorites. Sometimes we mix them with flowers that have no scent but have a pleasing shape. In the evening, these window boxes come into their own. The aroma of heliotrope and nicotiana is heightened, as is the scent of old-fashioned petunias, especially the white varieties. Fragrant moonflowers look like white morning glories and open at night, their saucerlike faces echoing their namesake.

Fragrant Ideas

Give your house a "clean sweep" with fragrant window boxes filled with plants that tease the senses. These suggestions will help get you started; feel free to experiment with combinations of your own.

For a LEMONY KITCHEN box, plant sweet basil, mints, lemon balm, lemon verbena, lemon thyme, and dill.

For a SCENTED NIGHTTIME window box, plant white nicotiana, white or purple heliotrope, moonflowers, sweet alyssum, and night-scented stock.

For an OLD-FASHIONED VICTORIAN scent box, plant lavender, pinks, white petunias, sweet peas, and jasmine.

For a MINT JULEP box, plant peppermint, spearmint, and pineapple mint. (Have a Bourbon rose blooming nearby for good measure!)

For a BAKERY WINDOW box, plant scented geraniums, chocolate cosmos, chocolate mint, and rosemary.

Opposite: Outside this kitchen window, the fragrance of white-flowered heliotrope and lemon verbena is carried on a breeze through the window screen to the kitchen. All the plants in this box are scented, but scented and unscented varieties can be mixed for much the same effect.

FRUITS & VEGETABLES

INSTEAD OF PLANTING the same old geraniums, make a statement by planting fruits and vegetables. They don't last long, but they're certainly fun for a few months until they're spent or transplanted into the yard. Our blueberry bushes in boxes yielded enough berries to top our cereal all summer, and supplied a season's worth of fruit salad as well. We've also had good luck with small-scale plantings of strawberries, onions, tomatoes, even baby watermelon vines. The key word is *experiment;* if it doesn't work out, there are plenty more plants to try.

Left: High-bush blueberries in painted garden boxes are the very definition of living color, with matching Elijah blue grass sprouting from the soil (detail opposite). Just by luck, they both require the same care—full sun in an area that is easily watered and also well drained. This setting is rustic, but the same pairing would look elegant flanking the entrance of a formal white house. In the fall, dig out the blueberries and give them permanent residence in the garden.

Opposite and right: Like musical notes on a scale, pots of tomato plants hang from the fence between a pair of espaliered pear trees. The 1950s coated-wire plant holders are all different, but each has a hook on the back for hanging on a fence slat. These holders were spotted at an antiques tailgate show, but similar designs can be found at garden centers. Above: Cherry tomatoes grow in a tin hat container on the chicken house door. The bite-size tomatoes are fed to the fryers when we gather their eggs each morning.

Window boxes can stray from their appointed sills with fine results. **Above left:** Ornamental onions—allium senescens glaucum—in a 1950s tin window box will flower light pink in July. **Above right:** A bed of straw draws the eye to concrete watermelon planters filled with pink geraniums and watermelon vines. The geraniums' color resembles the flesh of the water-melon. **Right:** A portable market basket filled with Quinault strawberries rolls from a sunny location to the party table. These particular strawberries are prolific, producing a second crop each season. To fill a large planter such as this, line it with a plastic bag and pour in packing peanuts until the container is three quarters full. Then add soil and plant strawberries on top.

WATER
BOXES

O N   A   H O T   S U M M E R   D A Y , even just the sight of water is cooling—sunlight reflecting off a water window box sitting below a window, casting patterns on the walls inside the house, or on a porch in front of the window, as beckoning as a pool or pond.

Many aquatic plants require full sun. Periodically replace the plants as necessary and replenish the water as it evaporates or gets cloudy. To control mosquito larvae that might be deposited in a water window box, add comets (a type of goldfish) or small koi. Before you add the fish, condition the water to eliminate

Left: Galvanized buckets on a garden bench spout water plants, including marsh marigold, umbrella plant, pennywort, dwarf papyrus, and parrot's feather. Opposite: A tumble of water hyacinths finds a refreshing spot in this water table, made by cutting out the top of an old table and inserting a galvanized trough with soldered seams so it holds water. The lip of the trough keeps it in place.

Exotic Aquatics

Water plants, with their showy flowers, spiky shafts, and liquid environment, never fail to intrigue. They grow in sun or shade, their roots trailing in the water, or they're planted in submerged pots of soil topped with stones and raised to the right height on stones or bricks.

Miniature floating plants are especially suitable for window boxes. Miniature water lilies (both hardy and tropical), miniature water lotus, marsh marigold, pennywort, dwarf papyrus, water fern, parrot's feather, water lettuce, Japanese sweet flag, water hyacinths, and water clover are all good choices. Upright plants such as umbrella plants, horsetail, rushes, water irises, dwarf cattail, calla lilies, pickerel rush, or any pointy grass make excellent edging for water window boxes.

There are hundreds of water plants to choose from, so ask your nursery for advice, or adapt information for ponds to the size of your aquatic window box.

chlorine and metals. Water window boxes offer limited space and should be regarded as a treat, not an ongoing arrangement. If you become enthralled with water plants, dig a garden pond, or put a larger container on your patio—an agricultural watering basin, galvanized cistern, wooden half barrel, large plastic bucket with a pump in the bottom, child's swimming pool, or two-foot-square black plastic containers used for mixing mortar are just some examples.

In the winter, put the fish in an indoor aquarium. Dispose of the plants, or store them, trimmed of foliage and set in plastic bags, in a box insulated with straw or pine needles in an unheated garage where they won't freeze. Tropical water lilies can be stored in damp sand at fifty-five degrees. We keep umbrella plants all winter in buckets of water on the greenhouse floor at fifty to eighty degrees.

Left: Plants in a gleaming galvanized box puts the "high-low" theory into practice: leggy water iris on **the left, a tall umbrella plant on the right, and low-lying water clover and water lettuce in the middle.**

Quick-Change Shelf

This easy-to-build box hangs on a wall, under a window, or on a gate or picket fence. Flowerpots fit into holes in the shelf, and can be changed to suit your mood. Use three identical plants, or make each pot different; herbs look great on one of these shelves near the kitchen or out on the deck. If company's coming and your party theme is blue, drop in pots of blue flowers. Or use three different white plants, which look especially pretty at night. Change pots and flowers each month or each season.

MATERIALS

For the shelf
Pine or cedar board, 29 inches long by 5^1/$_2$ inches wide (pine should be painted to protect the wood; cedar will age naturally and does not require paint)

For the brackets
Two pieces of wood, 7 inches by 10^1/$_2$ inches
Two wooden blocks, ^{3}/$_4$ inch high by 5^1/$_2$ inches long
Piece of #80 grit sandpaper

Using a jigsaw, cut three holes in the long board to fit the size of your flowerpots. Measure underneath the lip of the flowerpot so the pot slips into the hole and is held by the lip.

Drill a hole at the top back of each decorative bracket to mount it. Fasten the brackets to the shelf with nails. Glue and screw the small blocks beneath the shelf for support.

Finish the shelf by staining it first, then applying a coat of paint. When the paint is dry, sand lightly for a distressed finish. Screw or nail the shelf in place.

Zinnias and geraniums are ideal quick-change tenants.

89

AUTUMN PLANTS

coleus

chrysanthemum

rosemary

silver thyme

kale

fall pansies

asters

fall grasses

dahlias

small sunflowers

nasturtiums

bittersweet berries

zinnias

autumn crocuses

marigolds

goldenrod

wheat

pyracantha berries

thistle

pumpkins

Above: At a friend's house, a basket of Little Rudbeckia hangs on the door to the springhouse. Below: Milk thistles rise from a tin window box. Opposite: A fluffy window box is framed by cascading sweet potato vines. Overleaf: Purple fountain grass, gypsy sweet peppers, and coleus fill a painted bread box in our English cold frame.

EXTENDING THE SEASON

AUTUMN IS EASILY the favorite season around here, the golden days between summer and the holiday bustle. We shrug off summer and get back to work, but our blood runs more slowly, like the sap in the trees. The leaves spiral down to blanket the yard in a carpet of colors, and the last dried rosebuds cling to the bushes like good-luck pieces, reminding us that in the midst of change there are always new beginnings. Dean's sister calls from Tennessee and tells us she's eaten the last tomato from her garden in a white bread sandwich. We hang up and make the same lunch. For the time being, snowy days seem far away.

A few years ago we would have made ourselves very busy cleaning up the gardens. But now the beard of dried nasturtium vines and a tangle of ferns by the porch aren't clipped back until everything looks so ragged we can't ignore it any longer. We're content to watch the countryside unfold as we lean on our rakes in the backyard—for a few moments at least. Then we have jobs to do.

On a sharp sunny morning—the kind that comes after a day or two of hard rain—we add more bulbs to the yard: tall lavender alliums, white hyacinths, Apricot Beauty tulips because we love their color against the sage-green barn, and, always, tiny purple muscari to edge the boxwoods.

One of our newest acquisitions is an old cold frame from England, with a peak that ratchets up to let in air; we can only imagine the grand estate it came from. We use it to incubate bulbs that we've preplanted in window boxes, planters, and pots. For the lushest results, some bulbs are planted deep, others shallow—a double-digging effect in a window box. The potted bulbs are watered well and covered with straw or newspapers. They'll sleep in the cold frame until January or February, when we transfer them into the house for color.

Above: Fall cabbage adds a frill to the garden. Below: A volunteer pumpkin on the herb garden fence. Opposite: An arc of fresh-cut daisies seems to float in midair, suspended in a French flower holder that sticks to the window.

Natural fencing around the gardens looks especially beautiful this time of year, standing out as the plants recede. Supple apple twigs border the herb garden, poked into the ground in low six-inch arches, framed by rows of tall grasses, lavender, and oats. The green grasses are shooting out feathery plumes that change from maroon to beige as the weather gets colder. The Christmas trees we plant outside after each holiday extend the wind shelter along the property line beside the house.

Last year, the white beauty berries on the fences did so well that we went out and got some more—this time, to put around the hexagonal aviary in the white garden, where the doves live. We cover the sides of the aviary with Plexiglas to shelter the birds from the cold so they can live outside all winter.

As for the summer window boxes, some need a bit of fussing to make them right for fall. Anything that's still blooming is left to go the distance; we operate on the isn't-broken-don't-fix-it theory. Cuttings rooted late in the summer are mixed in, along with cold-tolerant herbs. The textures and shadings of thyme, parsley, winter savory, and sage set off cold-loving specimens like Supertunias, cabbage, asters, mums, brilliant marigolds, and verbena that bloom right up to a killing frost. Coleus are admired for their true autumn colors, but the watery stems mean they're always the first to go.

One year we took down all the window boxes and laid them by the greenhouse to rearrange and repot them, choosing a strong specimen from one, mixing it with a new plant from another, to make a better arrangement. But we've found it's easier just to run from box to box, transferring a bit of this and a bit of that until all of them look as we do this time of year—a little tired, but very hopeful, and ready for keen weather ahead.

COLORS OF AUTUMN

Soil Mixture

4 cups potting soil with vermiculite or perlite

1 cup sand

1 cup peat, compost, or manure

The soil in a window box loses many of its nutrients to the plants of spring and summer. Try this recipe to replenish the soil in the fall as you remove, replant, and rearrange your boxes.

THE EARTH SLOWS DOWN in September, and nature's fall palette spills through the foliage ringing the hills around the farm. In the garden, chill October nights snap coleus and cabbage to attention, their copper, chartreuse, and blazing ruby shades mixing with muted old gold and bronze. Now's the time we change the window boxes, reluctantly removing plants that are past their prime and replacing them with fresh. In other boxes, we start totally anew, bringing spots of color to the house, indoors and out.

If you live in an area that gets frost, as we do, the contest each autumn is to see which plants can go the distance. We've had luck with ox-eye daisies, thyme, rosemary, pansies, pinks, hellebores, silver artemesia, and scented geraniums. Keep deadheading the chrysanthemums to encourage new buds, and watch plants such as sedum and Boston ivy respond to cooler temperatures by turning colors, giving the garden a new look in the waning days of the year.

Opposite: Coleus, impatiens, nasturtiums, and marguerite sweet potatoes cling to a flat trellis that seems dimensional. Cocoa matting lines the wire planter to hold in the soil when the plants are watered.

Cleaning Up

In the fall we wash plastic window boxes with soapy water and a soft scrub brush, rinsing them well before we add new soil. Wooden boxes get sprayed with a hose and dried in the sun. If they need repainting, we sand them first, then slap on a coat or two of semigloss flat paint (we're partial to Benjamin Moore's Gloucester Sage). We reinstall most of them for fall and winter, storing a few in the shed until spring. We never bother to waterproof the boxes; they're not supposed to last forever. By the time they rot away, we're ready for new ones. Besides, untreated wood is better for Mother Nature.

Who says you need flowers for a knockout window box? Coleus in deep dark jewel colors—some of them almost black—are all the rage, and their foliage rivals any blossom. Here, pots of Bucksfoot Ruffled coleus, Solar Shadow coleus, Solar Storm coleus, and Solar Spectrum coleus squat in the recess of a scalloped shelf, juxtaposed against a dark shutter that intensifies their rich hues. The shelf has holes in the bottom for drainage. The scalloped edging is easy to make with a jigsaw.

Left: The hollow of a blue Hubbard squash holds northern sea oats and stonecrop sedum, which turns red as the weather cools. The squash makes a wonderful seasonal planter. Opposite: On a harvest table in the barn, flowering cabbages act as "bumpers" for cheerful marigolds and Golden Fleece goldenrod in a trim yellow box—a typical Thanksgiving centerpiece at Seven Gates. Straw wreaths, burlap, and gourds carry out the harvest theme. Overleaf: In the barn, sunflowers and ferns line up in a French window box, surrounded by the framed pages of a turn-of-the-century botanical scrapbook. Delicate and shallow, the late-nineteenth-century wirework box is four feet long, with a galvanized liner framed in wire. It can hold soil or separate pots of individual blossoms, as seen here. The pots are easily replaced for a fresh new look.

Opposite: Like a black-and-white snapshot, black sweet potato vines and white impatiens pack a kitchen window box near a trellis of fall-blooming clematis. Above right: Peter Pan cream zinnias, soft yellow-and-maroon coleus, and gazania daisies crowd a terra-cotta container. Below right: A twig box filled with Jennifer mums and Goldmine mums adds a rustic touch to the garden, and looks great indoors, too. Use tiny brads to hammer the twigs to the box; green twigs won't split. Overleaf: In a corner of the back garden, a pair of 1920s wrought-iron chairs boosts a box of rainbow swiss chard, the plants' rich colors backlit by the sun.

BIRD FEED BOX

Plants for BIRDS

milo
dwarf sunflowers
thistle
safflower
millet

THE BIRDS LOVE OUR GARDENS, and we love to welcome the birds. We sow bird feed in the spring, and by fall the dried plants offer fast food on the wing. Dwarf sunflowers go in the back of the bird feed box because they're the tallest, with milo in the middle and white proso millet across the front. Sunflower seeds, full of fat and protein, are a favorite of the chickadees, grosbeaks, titmice, jays, finches, and cardinals. Sparrows, juncos, and mourning doves go for the millet.

Planting one of these boxes is like preparing the soil for a new lawn. Sprinkle the seeds in the box and cover with a light coat of soil. Once-a-day misting keeps the soil damp until the seedlings are an inch high. We put ours in a quiet, sheltered window so the birds feel comfortable feeding there; they may crash-land if a window reflects an expansive scene or, because of its alignment, appears to lead through the house and out the other side. To break up these reflections, we line our windowsills with coleus cuttings, which root in milk bottles until spring. Hanging white paper cutouts in the window is another way to warn the birds.

Opposite: This bird feed box was planted in spring, watered all summer, and left to dry in the fall. Nutritious millet (far left) and sunflowers (left) are on the fast-food menu.

HARVEST
BOXES

SOME OF THE BEST CREATIONS are the unrehearsed boxes of fall, when enthusiasm for "arrangements" has been replaced by an urge to improvise. Simple wild weeds or roadside grasses can be the unexpected fill that brings a tired grouping back to life for a few more weeks. Chubby pumpkins, glossy eggplants, and multicolored squash take the place of expired plants. Look for pumpkins in colors other than the traditional orange, and vegetables you might not think of using outside, like garlic, parsnips, beets, and cauliflower, along with those staples of the autumn scene—Indian corn and feather corn with tiny garnet and gold kernels. Round shapes will counterbalance stalky plants trying to outrun the first killing frost with a final burst of energy.

Left: To fill out the bare spots after spent plants are removed at summer's end, we cut pyracantha branches, with their brilliant orange berries, and stick them in the dirt around still-thriving rosemary and creeping silver thyme. A sage-green pumpkin and a shock of feather corn on the window frame complete the picture. Opposite: A closer look at the rejuvenated box.

Harvesting for Fall

At this time of year, every part of the country has its own particular species madly blooming or going to seed. The roadsides around Seven Gates are absolutely brimming with foliage. If we see something unusual as we're driving along, we'll often pick it to bring home. We have a dark airy barn that's perfect for drying bouquets (hung upside down from the rafters). These dried plants make great fillers for fall window boxes that are a bit past their prime.

Some autumn boxes do fine without flowers altogether, taking advantage of the season's lush bounty instead. **Opposite:** A wheat stalk bouquet and ears of dried feed corn make a natural-tone display. Live grasses overflow the margins of the box for a hula-skirt effect. **Right:** Crookneck squash, butternut squash, bittersweet, and concrete pumpkins fill a hayrack padded with a thick bed of straw. This box can stay outdoors for weeks until the squirrels begin to feast on the squash.

Above left: Are they real? It's hard to tell that the leaves, pears, squash, Indian corn, and head of cabbage in this window box are actually made of fabric, as is the bittersweet twining around the little mirror on the wall.

Below left: Black-tipped wheat peeks out of a windfall of seckel pears—some real, some made of concrete—in a galvanized window box slim enough for a sill. Opposite: An arrangement of wild grasses, hydrangea, and red and yellow dogwood bursts from a painted sage-green box on the stepback cupboard in our kitchen. White gourds and pears take their place alongside, as if they'd just tumbled from the box.

HALLOWEEN
BOXES

O CTOBER MARKS A TURN in Maryland's weather, when the march toward winter truly begins. The frost is literally on the pumpkins, and on abandoned spider webs in the garden as well. Halloween was always our favorite holiday when we were children, and though we've given up wearing costumes, we still love to decorate the house. As dusk falls on All Hallows' Eve, we light candles inside the jack-o'-lanterns and gourds and hope for a dark night and a gentle wind so the shadows dance and the candlelight flickers.

You don't need an actual window box to get that all-in-a-row effect. Any flat surface, properly decorated, can be the stage for your displays. **Left:** A transom decorated window box style with warty gourds, greens, and clipped sedum draws attention to a vintage handmade Halloween dress hanging on the front door. The cut sedum stays fresh outdoors for a week. **Opposite:** Four hollowed-out pumpkins line up on the sill, a flowering kale planted in each one. Two pieces of wax paper cut to look like ghosts are taped to the window, backlit by candles burning inside the house.

Opposite: This polka-dot window box would delight the Addams Family. The wind-tossed "trees," which look as though a whirlwind just blew through, are two dead topiaries standing upside down, their root balls rinsed of dirt with a hose. Colorful accents include tufts of black Mondo grass, acorn squash so green it's almost black, and just-picked orange habanero peppers.

Right: A tall warty gourd with a cutout face would give any window box a Halloween air. This one was sawed in half crosswise with a band saw, scooped clean, and set atop a candle in the midst of meandering sweet potato vines, after frost did away with the white impatiens.

TERRARIUM
BOX

Materials

Potting soil
Crushed charcoal
Gravel or small stones
Peat moss
Assorted plants

mimosa, Norfolk Island pine, poly-
pody, asparagus fern, ficus, bird's
nest fern, fluffy ruffles fern, holly fern,
rattlesnake plantain, dwarf begonias,
cliff brake, salaginella, pellonia, and
twigs, nuts, leaves, moss, and small
pinecones for color and texture

A TERRARIUM BRINGS THE FOREST floor indoors. We have one
in the living room, where we can enjoy it all year-round. Any closed container
with a removable lid can be turned into one; ours has a galvanized liner that holds
an inch of stones topped with a sprinkling of charcoal. The charcoal is covered
with a thin piece of cloth and a mix of potting soil and peat moss.

A terrarium is happiest in diffused northern light. Moisture from the plants
and soil evaporates and collects on the sides of the terrarium and drips down like
rainfall, so beware of overwatering. Moisture evaporates more slowly when plants
are grown under glass. Mist the terrarium only when it starts to look dry—a
couple of times a month at most. If the terrarium fogs up, lift the lid for a day
or two to help prevent wilt and fungus.

VICTORIAN BOX

THE IDEA FOR THIS ENCRUSTED box came from an 1890s garden book, which showed turn-of-the-century ladies covering wooden boxes with an assortment of pinecones, twigs, acorns, walnuts, sticks, and curly grapevines. One hundred years later, at our own fin de siècle, it's time to revive the pastime and celebrate Victorian excess. The outside of the wooden box is covered with halved nutshells and whole pinecones glued on in a decorative pattern. We used walnut stain to give the box and decorations a uniform appearance, then varnished everything when the stain was dry.

This box is planted with Pteris ferns and golden celosia, a mix that could easily have been plucked straight from a nineteenth-century garden.

Left: The shapes of the decorations dictate the pattern that's created. Carpenter's glue holds the nutshells and pinecones in place. The twigs are easily attached with small brads. Opposite: The finished box is poised on a woodpile, the colors of the ferns and golden celosia (detail above left) standing out against this woodsy backdrop.

Copper Box

MATERIALS

Piece of light-gauge copper,
   18 inches by 32 inches
Tin snips
Hammer
Large nail
Four pieces of wire, each 26
   inches long
Dowel

We prize our copper window box for its looks as well as its function. Made from a piece of light-gauge copper available at sheet metal shops or hardware stores, the box has lace-up sides and drains from the corners, so holes on the bottom aren't necessary. If you plan to use the window box indoors, line it with plastic or build it to fit around a plastic liner.

To make the box, lay the copper on a flat surface. Using tin snips, cut a six-inch square from each of the four corners. Discard the corner pieces, and with the hammer and nail punch holes along the four L-shaped edges that result. Fold up the sides and secure each corner with wire from the bottom up, wrapping the wire ends around the dowel for a curlicue effect before removing the dowel.

To give the box an aged look, leave it outside for several months, or dab it with vinegar and baking soda, then rinse it off with a hose or rag when the right verdigris patina is achieved.

This box is planted with four lacy kale, but any mix of russet-toned fall plants will look great against the copper.

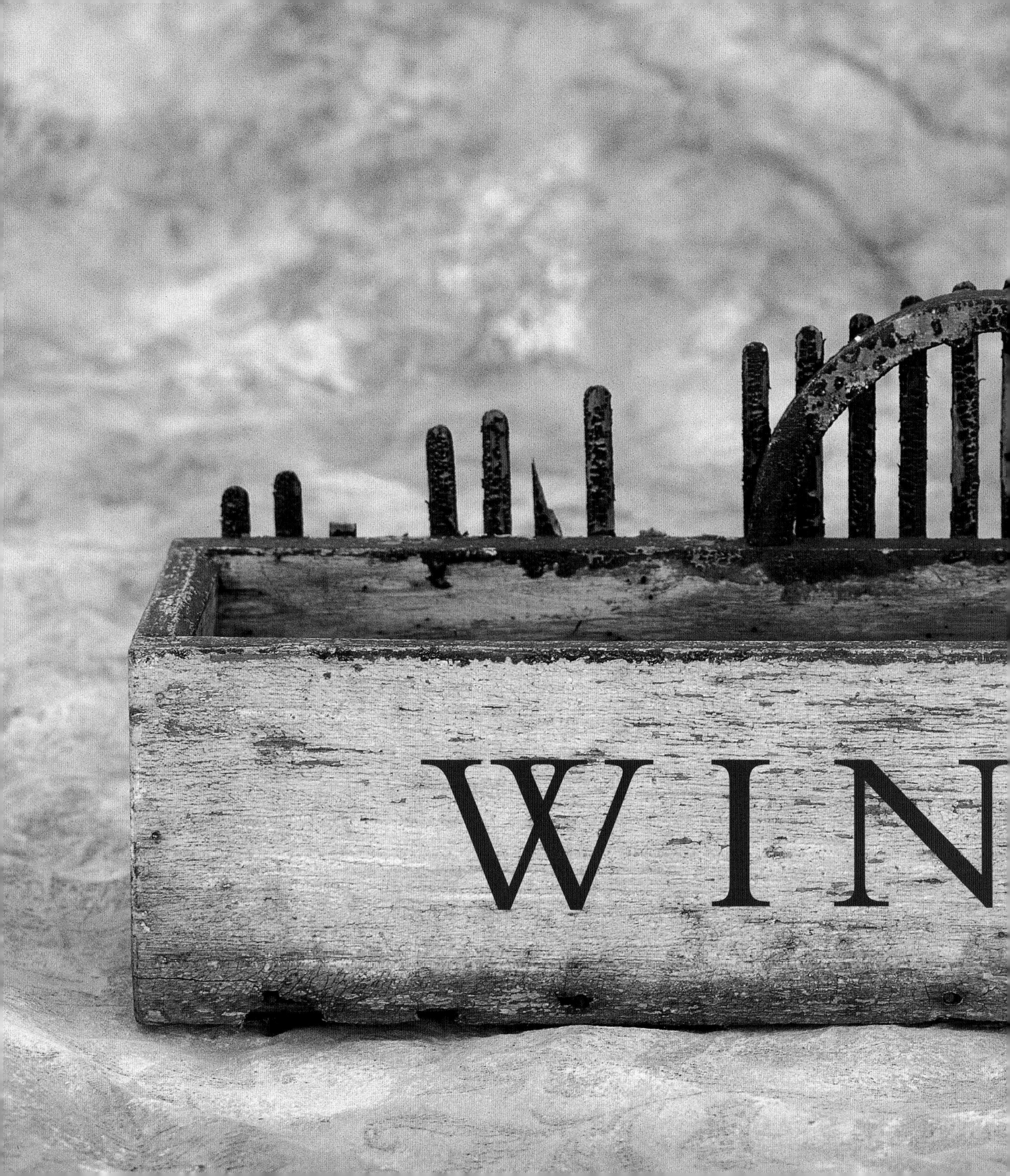
WIN

WINTER PLANTS

holly
rosemary
cyclamen
paperwhites
hyacinths
miniature roses
African violets
amaryllis
snowdrops
mistletoe
pine
begonias
bayberries
evergreens
boxwood
winterberries
Christmas cactus
moss
twigs
branches
red twig dogwood

Above and below: Snow and ice work their artistry on the bushes at Seven Gates Farm. Opposite: An Apple Blossom amaryllis emerges from a galvanized pot blanketed with moss.

CHANGES

THERE'S ICE ON THE BUSHES and snow in the gardens, but some corners of Seven Gates are oblivious to winter. Hyacinth, amaryllis, and ranunculus fill the greenhouse with perfume and color. In the cold frame, 250 tulip bulbs lie in a chill false spring. The tulips, potted in the fall, will soon put forth their first shoots, and the flowers will burst into multicolored madness sometime in the next month or two.

Our friend Rosita keeps a gardening notebook for inspiration, and after seeing hers, we've started one too. She writes down everything she orders by mail and buys at the nursery, and notes how each plant fared in the garden. Ours isn't as extensive, but includes drawings of fences and trellises, color copies of plants we like, and lists of plants we plan to buy in the spring. Starting a garden notebook is like starting a photograph album. You want to keep up with it, but sometimes the project slips away. For now we're keeping it at the kitchen table, where it's easy to fill in.

Seed shopping starts now, a carefully planned attack based on drawings of the gardens. We buy two of everything in case something dies. On our list this year: white proso millet, tomatoes, short Sunspot sunflowers, black broom corn for decorating, climbing nasturtiums and regular nasturtiums, morning glories, tall English wallflowers, sweet peas, white hyacinth beans, and purple hyacinth beans. We sit at the kitchen table and shuffle the seed packets like decks of cards. The future looks promising.

AT CHRISTMAS, WE DECORATE our collection of old white bottle brush trees with fresh herbs, tucking individual sprigs into the needles until each tree is lightly dressed. This small forest of fragrant trees will occupy the middle of the dining room table for several weeks.

Last Christmas we laid boughs of white pine and western red cedar on the outdoor windowsills, dog bone style, with the stems in the middle wired together and topped with a big burlap bow and sprigs of holly. The look of the beige burlap next to the greenery inspired our plans to paint our green-trimmed house beige instead of its current red.

Two years ago we discovered a little holly tree growing along the edge of the front porch; the holly from the windowsills that Christmas must have produced this diminutive offspring. The tree is a foot tall now, and we've transplanted it to the row of living Christmas trees on the north side of our property.

Above: Snapshots of winter, photographed in our gardens. Opposite: Adding red and green to a window box transforms it for the holidays. Here, cut holly and cotoneaster accent live boxwood bushes. Other choices are red crab apples, Canella berries, and dried rosebuds with green pine boughs, ivy, and pyracantha.

Above: A garden trug hooked to the windowsill, with a chicken-wire bottom and splint-oak staves, is filled with large pinecones and fluffy green boughs. Popcorn berries trim a square wire frame propped against the window. Opposite: A peek through the open door of a miniature indoor conservatory reveals myrtle topiaries and cyclamen enjoying the balmy climate.

On a warm day in February, we prune the apple trees to encourage fruit. At the tail end of March, when it seems as if winter will never end, we buy plants to lift our spirits. Some of our prettiest finds have come from the grocery store and Wal-Mart: bright pink cyclamen, yellow miniature roses, peace lilies with their stately white jack-in-the-pulpit–like flowers, small geraniums with chartreuse leaves, blooming calla lilies in pots, white azaleas, and antique pansies in old-fashioned colors such as apricot, pink, and soft butter yellow. The pansies go outdoors right away—only a real frost will kill them—and the others brighten up the indoors until the weather is warmer. We throw the plants into our shopping cart along with our winter survival foods—Oreos and Frappuccinos—and ponder the essential nourishment of both.

CHRISTMAS
BOXES

WINDOW BOXES FILLED WITH small evergreen trees, sprigs of holly, pinecones, and red berries are cheerful symbols of the season, and last outdoors through January. To make them, start by emptying dirt from boxes from the previous season and replacing it with something lighter, such as a layer of packing peanuts topped with sand. This makes a good anchor for branches and twigs, and provides some insulation for potted trees nested inside. If you have boxes of ivy, gather the tendrils into a sweeping garland like the ones on page 142. As a finishing touch, hang a wreath above each window box like a crown of green.

A sheltered area near the house may reflect enough warmth to carry a window box of potted rosemary or thyme through the winter. Left: A garden bench becomes the perfect pedestal for a box of young pine trees and delicate blossoming snowdrops (detail opposite). The snowdrops emerge from their creeping-evergreen groundcover like the lacy trim on a dress. They're self-sowing, and each year we dig up a clump or two outdoors, break them apart, and use them in our window boxes.

A classic winter window box of ivy looks good all year-round. No matter what the season, keep the ivy partly shaded so the leaves won't get sun-burned. Left: These boxes in front of a stone house in Shepherdstown, West Virginia, with their long tendrils of ivy, never fail to impress. At holiday time, the owners gather the tendrils into plump ivy garlands by pulling five or six strands together and inter-weaving them, twining them up and around and tucking in the ends to create a circle. Once the garlands are formed, the middle of the box can be decorated according to the season, with red berries or holly for winter, pansies in the spring, geraniums in summer, and a set of pumpkins in the fall. Above: During a warm spell, a box of rosemary and a silver germander topiary can survive a few days outside. The windowsill behind this box is heaped with holly tied with a big gold-webbed bow.

Living Wreaths

To brighten a window indoors or out, make a living wreath decorated with cotoneaster berries and ivy (opposite). Soak sheet moss in water. Lay a wire wreath form on the table and line it with the saturated sheet of moss, green side down. Fill with a mound of soil, more moss (green side up), and another wreath form. Wire the two forms together. Plant sprigs of rooted English ivy in the wreath, poking holes at the one o'clock, five o'clock, and ten o'clock positions. Add sticks of cotoneaster berries for color. Water the ivy whenever it looks dry.

Left: Red cotoneaster berries—ideal winter decorations because they last for months—punctuate fragrant green boxwood outside our dining room window; a living wreath hangs above. Watching from indoors is a cast-iron dove, an old finial from a garden gate. Right: During the holidays, we decorate an 1870s English stone birdbath with a pineapple resting on a bed of moss. The pineapple stays fresh-looking if the weather stays cold (a freeze-and-thaw cycle makes it mushy). White pine boughs silhouette the pyramidal base. Concrete or stone garden pieces can crack outdoors in winter, but this birdbath is sheltered on our front porch.

Right: Color and light make a yuletide centerpiece successful, and this arrangement is a winner. A begonia sits in fir boughs in a white trellis window box, surrounded by vanilla votives in galvanized flowerpots. Sparkly Victorian roping wound into yarn-like balls makes glittering orbs about five inches across. The decorations rest on a red-checked woolen blanket, beloved not only for its age, but for its warm color. Above: Boughs of fir with little pinecones as yet unopened; the red berries are wild rose hips.

With their long slender stems and spectacular flowers, amaryllis are the ballerinas of the flower world. They burst into bloom at the onset of winter, proclaiming that brilliance knows no season. All they ask is a warm, well-lit location and regular watering. Left: Belinda amaryllis crane their necks to the light. English holly trims the window. The gilded box was made by nailing brass decorations to the front and painting the entire box gold. The brass, often used to trim picture frames, is available at crafts shops. Opposite: Tightly held blossoms about to burst into triumphant display.

WINTER
RESTING BOX

WHEN THE CLOUDS GATHER in pleats above our orchard and a cold wind blows, it's time to make a resting box. With twisty sticks packed into sand, it has a contemplative, Zen-like quality; its simplicity reminds us to pause and embrace the dark side of the year rather than push for spring. On an ordinary day it looks artistic. Add the sparkle of snow and ice and the effect is magical.

This resting box is filled with curly pussy willow. For a stark white effect, choose birch branches or ammobium branches. For unusual shapes, use various lengths of Harry Lauder's walking stick branches. Line up the sticks with taller branches in back, and let some curl down in front. Snow gives the box a crystalline look, but if the forecast is clear, help nature along by spraying the box with water on a cold night, then again first thing in the morning. Or aim the sprinkler on the boxes on a cold night: The sticks and twigs will turn into artful icicles.

Left and right: Instead of denying the bleakness of the season, why not point it up? This austere window box of sticks, looking like a masterpiece by Edward Scissorhands, best expresses the iciness in the air. A box like this one is an easy alternative to more elaborate winter arrangements and can be as calming as a Japanese garden, both to make and to contemplate. Top the sand with moss to give the box a finished look.

New Year's Eve Box with Candle Holder

To celebrate a new year, make a high-wattage all-white window box for indoors. This antique white box trellised with Popsicle sticks contains two dwarf cypresses and a plethora of popcorn berries that shine like a million little lightbulbs. The stems of the branches are stuck in the dirt. To focus attention on the box, drape white Christmas lights on several larger trees below it. Making the wire candle holder that hangs in the window is a simple project.

MATERIALS

Spool of 18-gauge tie wire
Wire cutters
Candle
A ½-inch dowel

Cut a piece of wire three feet long. Lay a candle in the middle of it, then wrap the wire around the candle five times. Pull up the loose ends of the wire into a circle and twist together at the top, leaving enough wire to wrap around the dowel. Twist the wire around the dowel to make a spring on each side, then remove the dowel and clip the wire ends. Hang the wire from a nail above the window box.

White BERRIES

POPCORN BERRIES

(also called tallow berries or Tyler tree berries)

SNOWBERRIES

(symphoricarpos albus)

BAYBERRIES

(myrica caroliniensis)

JAPANESE BEAUTY BERRIES

(also come in purple and light purple)

STEP BY STEP

153

VALENTINE'S DAY BOX

The Language of FLOWERS

RED ROSE
a pure heart

WHITE LILAC
youthful innocence

BLUEBELL
constancy

RED POPPY
consolation

BLUE VIOLET
faithfulness

CABBAGE ROSE
ambassador of love

**Right and opposite:
A little wooden box with
carved designs might have
been a child's jewelry box
long ago. Filled with roses,
it is a thoughtful token of
love, paired with an antique
garden-theme valentine.**

FOR A SPECIAL VALENTINE, make an indoor window box to take the place of an ordinary bouquet or formal arrangement. Choose miniature red roses, or any other flower that carries a sentimental meaning. Finish with heart-shaped ivy or a cloud of baby's breath. To find the right box, search tag sales and antiques shops. We found this hinged wooden box, with incised hearts and stars and a heart-shaped mirror inside the lid, at a flea market. You can also make your own wooden box and decoupage it with antique valentines or cutout hearts. If your box isn't waterproof, line it with a sheet of plastic or a preformed plastic liner before you add the plants.

FORCING BULBS

Soil Mixture

3 cups sand
3 cups peat moss
2 cups vermiculite
1 cup horticultural charcoal

Combine all the ingredients to make a perfect medium for forcing most kinds of bulbs.

GET A HEAD START ON MAY by forcing spring bulbs in an indoor box. Hyacinths, paperwhites or tête-à-tête narcissus, tulips, crocuses, grape hyacinths, and amaryllis all bring a shot of bright color to any room and add sweet fragrance to the air. Create a portable window box to move from room to room. Or place a row of containers side by side on a table or the floor. You can even position a dry sink or bucket bench near a window, with pots of forced blossoms resting in a bed of straw within the recessed top.

Right: Belinda amaryllis start their journey in a gold-painted box on the windowsill. Several weeks later, they'll burst into spectacular bloom (see page 148). **Overleaf:** A table in front of a window is the perfect place for a trio of Apple Blossom amaryllis in galvanized tins. Like children, amaryllis bloom in their own time; the one in the middle bloomed short. On the garden chair, a brown linen pillow with handwritten inscriptions resembles a vintage burlap sack for bulbs. The flower names were written on the pillow with permanent brown calligraphy ink and a small thin paintbrush.

Paperwhite Wreath

Don't throw the bulbs and foliage away after your paperwhites have blossomed—use them to make a wreath for spring. First, pull the paperwhites out of their container after they have bloomed. Shake off the stones and clip off the spent blossoms, leaving the long green leaves and whiskery roots intact.

Fasten a bulb and leaves to a sixteen-inch grapevine or straw wreath form by wrapping green florist's wire or hemp around the top of the bulb, just at the base of the foliage. Then wrap and tuck the long green leaves around the wreath form. Add another bulb and continue wrapping and tucking all around the wreath, spacing the bulbs out and wiring or tying where necessary to hold things in place.

Opposite: Hyacinths are among the easiest bulbs to force. They can be forced in dirt or in a narrow-necked forcing glass that supports the bulbs above water. The 3-3-3 forcing formula is easy to remember: three weeks in the dark so roots can form; three days of strong north light once the sprouts are three inches long. Then the bulbs can be transferred to full sun. Above: Hyacinths that have reached their goal bask in a straw-filled dry sink near a sunny window.

Forcing Paperwhites

Paperwhite narcissus, with a marvelous heady scent, are easy to force into bloom between October and March. It takes about five weeks for the blossoms to appear; once they do, they'll thrive in a cool room. Plant in early October for Thanksgiving bloom, and in November for Christmas. Plant every two weeks for a continuous supply of blossoms; the bulbs will bloom faster as spring approaches.

This whitewashed wooden window box has a primitive picket fence made of lathe. Because the paperwhites' bending stems tend to get heavy and flop over as they grow, we made V-shaped cuts in the corner pickets and laid twigs across as supports.

water to just reach the base of the bulbs. Top with sheet moss. Place the window box in a cool dark place for two to three weeks to encourage root growth and subsequent sprouting.

When pale green shoots are three to four inches tall, bring the container to bright indirect light for a day or two, then move it to a sunny window where the temperature is cooler than seventy degrees. The paperwhites will bloom in two to three weeks. Stems will bend toward the light; rotate the container each day to keep them straight. Monitor the water level so the roots are not exposed.

MATERIALS

Window box
Plastic window box liner
Packing peanuts
River gravel
Paperwhite narcissus bulbs
Sheet moss

Fit a pretty wooden window box with a plastic liner. Fill half the container with packing peanuts, then top with river gravel.

Set upright bulbs on top of the gravel about an inch apart, anchoring them with a few more pebbles. Roots will grow down to hold the paperwhites upright. Add

WINTER CONSERVATORY

Plants for an INDOOR GREEN-HOUSE

African violets
geraniums
ferns
succulents
orchids
flowering bulbs
cyclamen

Opposite: A mix of Gothic and Federal styling characterizes this one-of-a-kind conservatory. The 1920s cast-iron eagle once presided over a gas station in Oklahoma. With the proper light and temperature, any plant that abhors a draft and likes humidity will be happy here all winter, like the cyclamen (detail right).

WE BUILT THIS HOUSELIKE CONSERVATORY for two reasons: Our house is drafty in winter, and we enjoy the lift that colorful house plants give this time of year. It resembles not only our greenhouse out back but also the glass houses and orangeries found in nineteenth-century botanical gardens, where fruit and other tender plants were grown. Our conservatory babies myrtle topiaries, cyclamen, and orchids until spring, when the myrtles go back outside. Set in a place of prominence—in this case, a south-facing bay window—it looks as stately as any other piece of furniture. The top, incidentally, is vented to control heat and humidity.

Shard Box

Broken china plates give this wooden window box its charming crazy-tea-party quality. Look for old or damaged plates at antiques malls, flea markets, or garage sales. You're sure to find some in your favorite colors that are reasonably priced.

Covering this window box took five chipped brown transferware and ironstone plates found at a flea market. Rather than simply smashing the plates, cut them into shards using tile nippers to create more generous pieces. If your box is going to hold flowerpots instead of loose dirt, as this one does, measure the pots before you buy or build the box.

The shard window box is designed to be used indoors or in a sheltered spot outside, such as a covered porch.

MATERIALS

Wooden window box
Tile nippers
Plates
Plastic bucket of premixed
    ceramic tile mastic
Putty knife
Sanded floor grout
A 6-by-6-inch piece of bubble wrap
Small sponge

Spread your work surface with brown kraft paper or another protective covering. Using the back of the nippers or a hammer, crack each plate to give the nippers a starting point, then use the nippers to cut the plate into random-size pieces.

Spread mastic on the back of each piece of china with a putty knife. Press the pieces onto the box, arranging them in any pattern you choose; leave small spaces between each piece for grout. Let the pieces dry for twenty-four hours, or at least overnight. (The back of the box isn't visible, so we didn't cover it.)

With a paint-stirring stick, mix the grout with water to a workable consistency. Using the same stick, lay little dabs of grout on the front and sides of the box.

Use the bubble wrap to push and smooth grout in between the china pieces until the grout is fairly smooth. Let dry forty-five minutes to an hour, until a white film appears.

Moisten a sponge and wring it out so it is just damp, not wet. Wipe over the grout, smoothing it as you go. Keep rinsing the sponge as you work, using a plastic bucket instead of the sink so you don't clog the plumbing. Continue wiping until the white film on the shards is gone. You may have to do this two or three times, every fifteen minutes or so, until the pieces are clean. The grout will dry very hard within a couple of hours.

When the box is finished, fill it with potted plants. We used dusty miller and cyclamen.

STEP BY STEP

GLASS BOXES

BEFORE WINTER ARRIVES, we bring our lead-and-glass boxes inside from the garden. Placed on a windowsill, these cloches, as they are called, capture the sunlight like little greenhouses. They create the perfect environment for growing African violets; the plants sit inside on metal trays. You can also germinate pots of different grasses under glass, or show off a variety of mosses. Each glass box is narrow enough to rest on a mantel, where antique flowerpots or any other precious collectible can be displayed, just as the Victorians kept dried flowers under glass to show them off and discourage dust. As a bonus, the glass box acts as a prism when the sun shines, casting rainbows on the wall.

Left: African violets bloom in the window, the pale north light of winter amplified by a glass-and-lead "hothouse" cloche. Opposite: The cloche keeps violets at just the right temperature. If moisture begins to collect inside, the humidity can be vented by raising one side on a spool, small clay pot, or stone. Upending the cloche for a few hours will also clear the interior. Overleaf: A lichen-covered stone sink is filled with concrete pears.

Growing African Violets

- place plants in low light or indirect sunlight

- avoid drafts

- place plants in a saucer, then water from the bottom

- water with warm water, no more than once a week

- don't let plants sit in water

- avoid wetting foliage

- feed with a 10-60-10 liquid fertilizer, diluted as directed

- pinch off flowers as they fade

- repot when the stem is one inch above the dirt (about once a year)

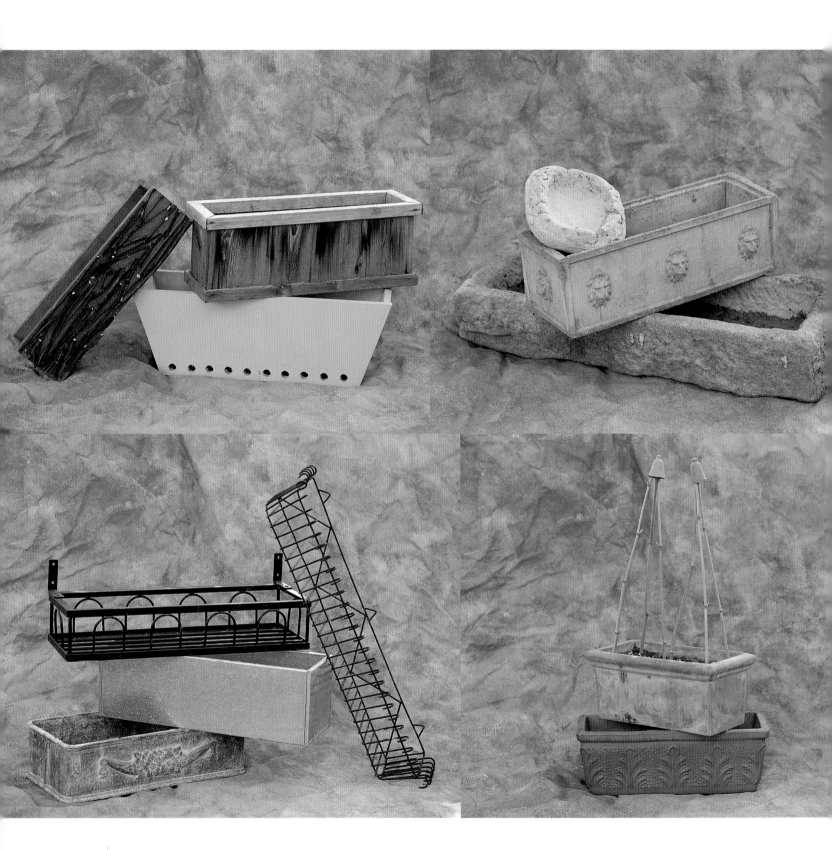

CONTAINERS

In general, plain and unadorned are best—often just a simple scallop will do. The flowers and foliage are the main attraction; when they cascade over the sides, they often hide the box itself.

WOOD

Will last from two to ten years, depending on the wood, but eventually disintegrates. Painted cedar boxes or unpainted redwood, teak, and cypress containers will last for many years; the unpainted boxes will age to a natural patina.

STONE AND CONCRETE

Ideal for porches, patios, and entrances to a garden, but they must be securely supported on elevated areas such as windowsills. Be sure the texture of the plant looks good with the texture of the container; boxwood looks great, ferns soften hard edges. Aim for contrast.

METAL

Absorbs heat, so save for heat-resistant plants in shady or semi-shady areas. In areas of heavy rainfall, wire containers drain quickly, so a plant's roots don't get soggy. A lining of moss or cocoa matting prevents the soil from washing away.

TERRA-COTTA

Plants in terra-cotta pots require frequent watering because the water evaporates quickly through the clay. Because of their weight, these containers must be securely fastened to a sill. They blend well with stone or brick.

Anthropologie
1700 Sansom Street, 6th Floor
Philadelphia, PA 19103
(800) 309-2500
www.anthropologie.com
garden accessories (stores nationwide)

Around the Bend
Rick and Denise Pratt
7883 Cleveland Road
Wooster, OH 44691
(330) 345-9585
www.aroundthebendwillowfurni ture.com
willow and twig boxes and planters

Foltz Pottery
225 North Peartown Road
Route 1
Reinholds, PA 17569
(717) 336-2676
www.foltzpottery.com
redware flowerpots

Frenchwyres
P.O. Box 131655
Tyler, TX 75713
(903) 597-8322
wire window boxes, plant stands

Great Stuff by Paul
10 North Carroll Street
Frederick, MD 21701
(888) 729-4548
European, Canadian, Chinese, and United States garden antiques

Hobensack & Keller
P.O. Box 96
57 West Bridge Street
New Hope, PA 18938
(215) 862-2406
fine garden appointments: lead, wrought iron, stone, terra-cotta

Kinsman Company
P.O. Box 428
Pipersville, PA 18947
(800) 733-4146
www.kinsmangarden.com
hayracks, terra-cotta planters, window boxes

Nathan's Forge, Ltd.
3476 Uniontown Road
Uniontown, MD 21158
(877) 848-7903
www.nathansforge.com
iron window boxes

Plow & Hearth
P.O. Box 6000
Madison, VA 22727
(800) 494-7544
www.plowhearth.com
cedar window boxes

Restoration Hardware
(800) 816-0901
galvanized boxes, containers, wire window boxes (stores nationwide)

Smith & Hawken
P.O. Box 8690
Pueblo, CO 81008-9998
(800) 776-3336
www.smithandhawken.com
window boxes, containers (stores nationwide)

Windowbox.com
3821 S. Santa Fe Avenue
Vernon, CA 90058
(888) 427-3362
www.windowbox.com
broad selection of window boxes and mounting hardware

SEEDS, BULBS, & PLANTS

All suppliers listed offer catalogs.

Brent and Becky's Bulbs
7900 Daffodil Lane
Gloucester, VA 23061
www.brentandbeckysbulbs.com
spring and summer flowering bulbs

Burpee Seed Company
300 Park Avenue
Warminster, PA 18991
(800) 888-1447
www.burpee.com
plants, bulbs, seeds

Gurney's Seed and Nursery Co.
P.O. Box 4178
Greendale, IN 47025
(513) 354-1491
www.gurneys.com
bird seed mix, catalog

Jackson & Perkins
P.O. Box 1028
Medford, OR 97501
(877) 322-2300
www.jacksonandperkins.com
plants

Johnny's Selected Seeds
955 Benton Avenue
Winslow, ME 04901
(207) 861-3901
www.johnnyseeds.com
heirloom and unusual flowers and vegetables

John Scheepers
23 Tulip Drive
P.O. Box 638
Bantam, CT 06750
(860) 567-0838
www.johnscheepers.com
bulbs

J. W. Jung Seed Co.
335 S. High Street
Randolph, WI 53957
(800) 247-5864
www.jungseed.com
seeds, plants

Lilypons Water Gardens
P.O. Box 10
Buckeystown, MD 21717-0010
(800) 999-5459
www.lilypons.com
aquatic plants

Thompson & Morgan
P.O. Box 1308
Jackson, NJ 08527
(800) 274-7333
www.thompson-morgan.com
English seeds

Van Bourgondien Bros.
245 Route 109
P.O. Box 1000
Babylon, NY 11702
(800) 622-9997
www.dutchbulbs.com
plants

Wayside Gardens
1 Garden Lane
Hodges, SC 29695
(800) 845-1124
www.waysidegardens.com
seeds, plants

White Flower Farm
P.O. Box 50
Route 63
(800) 503-9624
www.whiteflowerfarm.com
bulbs, plants, gifts

ACKNOWLEDGMENTS

As always, it takes a team to produce a beautiful book, and we are grateful to have such very talented people working with us.

Thank you to
Mary Sears, more a sister to us than a colleague, for her wonderful words.
Anne Gridley and Gary Graves for their beautiful photography and many trips to our farm, for which we are so appreciative.
Susi Oberhelman, for her discerning eye and great style.
Our editor, Laurie Orseck, and Ann Bramson at Artisan, for giving us great freedom on this book. The front gate is always open.

Thank you to all the gardeners who shared their window boxes with us:
Rosita Ray, a true gardener in every sense of the word.
Nancy Waltz at Surreybrooke Farm
Jan Bender and Amy Fries at The Village Green Shop
Betsy Callahan in Nantucket
Yvon Le Fichant
Kinsman Company in Pennsylvania

The artists and friends who shared their work with us:
Jeanette McVay (concrete pears and pumpkins), a true friend who is always looking for garden antiques for us.
Norma and Jennifer Schneeman (fabric vegetables), who continually amaze us.
Nick Drzayich (spice box), a talented woodworker.
Rick and Denise Pratt (twig box), the best around for willow work.
Steve and Mary Petlitz (tin hat and thistle window box), wonderful tinwork.
Nathan's Forge (hand-forged window box), a blacksmith extraordinaire.

We'd also like to single out Potomac Farms Nursery in Shepherdstown, West Virginia, and Timmy, Darby, and Melanie Zimmerman at Thanksgiving Farms Nursery in Buckeystown, Maryland, who grow new and different plants each year, for everyone.

Our heartfelt thanks to Mary Emmerling for fourteen years of support, and for always being there.
Debbie Ray for our wonderful tour of England. We will never forget it.
Emelie Tolley, who never fails to have a good word for us.
June Wollard, who always keeps us in stitches.
Ned and Gwen Foltz, for great friendship, food, and redware.
Gina Rosenwald, for keeping us in touch.
Howard Souders and Morgan Anderson, for bringing us treasures.
Jeanne and Edie and Brody, our favorite afternoon visitors.
And to our families, who we don't see enough of.

Thank you to the wonderful antique-, gift-, and garden shops who have always supported our work, and to all the people we've heard from who keep giving us rave reviews and continually supply kind comments and support. You're the reason we continue to do what we do.